‖ THE WORLD OF MUSIC ‖

Folk Music

Published by Creative Education
P.O. Box 227
Mankato, Minnesota 56002
Creative Education is an imprint of The Creative Company.

DESIGN AND PRODUCTION BY zeno design

PHOTOGRAPHS BY Corbis (Nubar Alexanian; Bettmann; Henry Diltz; Peter
Johnson; Papilio; Roger Ressmeyer; Peter Turnley; Tony Wilson-Bligh), Getty
Images (Frank Driggs Collection; Frank Seifert; Three Lions; Weegee (Arthur
Fellig)/International Centre of Photography)

library of congress cataloging-in-publication data

Riggs, Kate.
Folk music / by Kate Riggs.
p. cm. — (World of music)
Includes index.
ISBN 978-1-58341-566-5
1. Folk music—United States—History and criticism—Juvenile literature. I. Title.

ML3551.R54 2008
781.62—dc22   2006102983

First edition

9 8 7 6 5 4 3 2 1

Folk

MUSIC

KATE RIGGS

CREATIVE EDUCATION

Folk music is the earliest kind of music. It is like telling a story through a song. For hundreds of years, people learned the songs by listening to them. They did not write anything down.

Many folk songs came from Africa

Then people wanted to write folk music down. Some people went all over the world in the 1800s. They looked for different kinds of folk music. They wanted to write down music from lots of places.

African folk music uses a lot of drums

The guitar is a folk music instrument. It is made out of wood and has six strings. Folk musicians (*mew-ZIH-shuns*) use other string instruments, too. They play fiddles. They play banjos, too.

A person's voice is the main instrument in folk music.

A guitar has six strings

Many people in the United States liked folk music. They liked songs from places like Africa and Europe (*YOO-rup*). They used parts of these songs to make new folk music.

Folk musicians do not always sing for money. Many of them sing or play just for fun.

Some folk musicians play pipes

Pete Seeger was a famous folk singer. He sang songs about war. He sang songs about people who were poor. People liked Bob Dylan and Joan Baez (*BY-ez*), too. Their songs changed the way people thought about things.

Pete Seeger made playing the banjo popular.

Folk singer Pete Seeger

People in the state of New York loved folk music. Folk groups liked playing there, too. There were always lots of folk singers in New York.

Folk music can be played anywhere

But some people in other places did not like folk music. They did not like to hear what folk singers had to say. Some folk singers got in trouble for singing their music.

Some folk singers used music to protest against things they did not like.

Singer Joan Baez at a protest

A kind of music called rock and roll helped change folk music. Rock and roll music was loud. It was fast, too. New folk-rock singers played their instruments louder. They used faster beats. Lots of people liked the new sounds of folk-rock.

Simon and Garfunkel was a popular folk-rock group in the 1970s.

Folk music is still popular today

Some folk singers have lots of fans. Some play for a few people in a coffee shop. Folk music can be made by anyone. It can be made anywhere. All it takes is a voice and a song!

"This Land Is Your Land" is a folk song by Woody Guthrie.

Peter and Paul, of the group Peter, Paul and Mary

GLOSSARY

banjos instruments that people play by picking the strings with their fingers

fiddles small instruments with strings; also called violins

folk-rock a mix of folk and rock music

instruments things people play to make music

protest to speak up about things a person does not like

Joni Mitchell was a popular folk singer

INDEX